CW00838943

Thoughts
for Stressful Times

Lionel & Patricia Fanthorpe

BISHOPSGATE PRESS

This book is dedicated to all my friends in JUMBO,
a bikers' charity which arranges happy and exciting
outings for handicapped children and their loving
carers. In so doing, JUMBO provides a wonderful
antidote to stress.
"Ride safe, boys and girls!"

British Library Cataloguing in Publication Data
Fanthorpe, Lionel and Patricia
Thoughts and Prayers for Stressful Times

All enquiries and requests relevant to this title
should be sent to the publisher Bishopsgate
Press Ltd., Bartholomew House, 15 Tonbridge
Road, Hildenborough, Kent TN11 9BH.

Printed by Lanes Ltd.,
16 Patricia Way, Pysons Road Industrial Estate,
Broadstairs, Kent CT10 2LF.

Contents

Foreword
by Canon Stanley Mogford, MA

Bridge builders are people to admire. In one sense, they act as peace makers between nations at war, and individuals at loggerheads with one another. Their presence and words are like silken cords drawing old enmities into understanding and harmony. Jesus called them, "Children of God" and we can never have enough of them.

In the literal sense, bridge builders design and construct bridges, not between people, but over ravines and rivers. We owe them much. Sometimes their bridges are so suspended, they look, to the untutored eye without the expected means of support. They will have to bear the stresses of age, climate, winds, and the weight of ever increasing traffic. Such builders never put people's lives at risk. They design them not merely to resist a known weight, not even double that weight, but, as far as can ever be known with any certainty, all possible stresses and strains by which they could be tested. They build them to last and they do.

The human being, too, is built to resist many pressures. Stress seems to be a fact of life now and no doubt it has always been so. There are burdens to be borne, greater, of course, for some than for others, but they are always there, threatening and insistent. Job speaks for all under strain when he says: "Man is born unto trouble as the sparks fly upwards". However, we can take heart, as Job took heart. Like the bridges, we are built to be strong: we are made to resist the worst of our strains and stresses. Made by God, in his image, endowed by God with His Grace we have His Power to use - if we have wisdom enough to seek it.

Identifying pressure is certain to vary with the individual. For many it will be at its worst in the work

5

place. A generation or so ago, employment, once started, was deemed to be assured. Individuals entered from school or college and remained with the one company until retirement and a gold watch. Now it's a matter of continuous appraisal, short term renewable contracts and a constant threat of redundancy and unemployment. People now seem to work under fear. The stress of the work place is often exacerbated by stress at home. For those harassed at work, even the family home shows no sure place of recreation and peace. In fact, stress is everywhere. It is as great a menace to 21st Century life as the terrible diseases that once ravaged and decimated the people of earlier centuries.

By God's Grace there is help to be found. Some of that help we can find within ourselves. God has so made us that we are stronger and firmer than all the cares and anxieties crowding into our lives. We survive and they perish. St Teresa was right, "Be not afraid . . . Everything passes". We have great reserves of strength on which we can call. We are natural survivors and come through the worst, if not unscathed, at least unbroken.

Others also are there for us and are ever anxious to help. This book has been written for this very purpose. It is full of wisdom and written in love. The words of Jesus are reflected everywhere in every page of it.

"Come unto me all ye that are weary and heavy laden; and I will give you rest."

Of course no book can do what lay in the power of Jesus of Nazareth. It is written to help as best it can and it will.

Canon Stanley Mogford
Cardiff, 2001

Introduction

The unpleasant sensations which we describe as *stress* seem to be very personal and individualistic things. We all have different vulnerabilities to it. Human beings face life wearing different types of mental and spiritual armour - and no matter how good it is, we all have our weak points *somewhere*. The hero who can face down a hostile mob or swim through white water to save a drowning companion without feeling in the least stressed, may be unable to touch a spider without risking a nervous breakdown. The carefree gardener who doesn't even notice that her tool-shed is full of spiders may not be able to tackle an assertive and dominant neighbour whose cat is digging up cherished plants on a regular basis. Neither is in the least superior or inferior to the other: just *different*. We are as clearly distinguished from one another by our idiosyncratic stress triggers and stress thresholds as we are by our height, weight or hairstyle.

That's the first thing we should consider when tackling the problems that stress causes. To be stressed is to be human. Coping with it and carrying on with our lives in spite of it is what makes us the worthwhile men and women that God designed us to be, wants us to be, and will enable us to be - if only we will ask for His help.

If a car, computer, TV or washing machine goes wrong, most of us have to call in an expert to put it right again. The engineer who comes to our rescue knows more about the thing than we do, so we naturally trust him, or her, to get it going for us. God made this whole awe-inspiring universe. He also made each one of us as a unique, special and greatly loved human being to live in it and enjoy it. God knows infinitely more about us and our amazing environment than the wisest man or woman can ever hope to learn. When stress seems to be overwhelming us, we need God's help first, last and always. He knows exactly what you and I need to solve our particular stress problems: the Divine Doctor always has just the right anti-stress prescription for everyone - whatever their personality style, and whatever the circumstances that are causing their specific stress problems.

The Stress of Isolation

There are times when being alone - or feeling alone even at the heart of a bustling crowd - can produce desperate feelings of stress. It sometimes occurs to us that we are totally isolated, that we have no resources but ourselves, and that our own inner strength is no match for an increasingly hostile and threatening environment.

One way of overcoming this kind of negative feeling is to remember that it is only a feeling. It's just a mood, a subjective mental experience. It isn't real. The next step is to ask ourselves about the significant people in our lives, the people we love, the people who love us, and the people who depend upon us. No matter how separate, isolated and alone we may feel, the reality is that we are bound to them, and they are bound to us. The third step is to ask ourselves about things - material or abstract - which matter to us: antiques, paintings, our collection of stamps or coins, the team we support, the dishes we cook, the poems we write, the car we drive, or the Harley Davidson we ride. What about the good causes that matter to us: our Christian faith, our political and social ideals, our determination to help the old, the frail, the mentally or physically challenged? We are an inseparable part of our ideals and they are an inseparable part of us. We may sometimes feel the stress of isolation - but we are, in fact an essential thread in God's tightly woven, supportive social fabric.

Always with God

In darkest night, or brightest day,
Via city crowds, or trackless way,
In deepest caves of marbled stone:
God loves us. We are not alone.
The ones we love, the cause we take,
Woven with cords which cannot break;
Friends and companions, sisters, brothers -
Thank God for love: thank God for others.

Prayer

Loving Heavenly Father, Son and Holy Spirit,
help us to understand that as You, our God,
are Three Persons in One glorious and mysterious
Triune Godhead, so we, your creation, are
made to belong to You and to one another in loving
and eternal fellowship.
Amen.

The Stress of Over-Crowded Days

There are times when too many things happen simultaneously. The harder we try to deal with them, to juggle appointments, to delegate, to refer, the pressure continues to build up relentlessly until it becomes dangerously stressful.

With dynamic electronic information and communication explosions going on all around us at an ever-accelerating pace, the stress of trying to cope with it all seems to get heavier every day.

The first answer is an irrepressible, unsinkable sense of humour. One person simply cannot do ten people's work. It's ridiculous to think that we can, and ridiculous things are funny - so laugh at the crazy impossibility of it all, but go on trying even while you're laughing at your own valiant efforts to square the circle or to lift yourself up by your own shoelaces. The next step is to prioritise. All the jobs you've got lined up are important, but some are immediate and vital, others can wait a while if they have to. Sort them out and then do the most urgent and important one first. The highest priority is always to help those in greatest need for the sake of the God who loves them.

Too Much, Too Many, Too Fast

The job confronting me today
Was always wanted yesterday,
While those for whom I ought to pray
Are waiting still.

The closing dates and deadlines all
Join in a loud, demanding call.
Although my back's against the wall
I'm fighting still.

For He who came to save our race
Gives hard-pressed warriors breathing space.
From Him we hear the words of grace,
His: "Peace, be still."

Prayer

Lord of everlasting peace, eternal calm
and unending tranquillity, grant us the
grace to understand that you are always
there to protect and support us, and to
supply us with that quietness and confidence
wherein true and enduring strength is to be found.
Amen.

The Stress of Waiting

The ordeal of the job interview is stressful enough, but waiting for the result is often worse. Sitting important examinations is also very stressful, but waiting for the results is more so. How do we get around this waiting-stress problem which invades so many areas of our 21st Century life?

One tried and trusted strategy is to pretend to ourselves that we are experiencing something much more pleasant. We aren't in the candidate's waiting room after that all-important promotion interview: we're waiting for the theatre to open so that we can watch a new show we've been looking forward to for months. We're having a picnic with friends and waiting for the kettle to boil.

Another technique is to wipe the whole experience from our memories. The interview never happened. We are not expecting any important decisions to be made. Life is very tranquil. The steady, reassuring pattern of familiar everyday events goes quietly and smoothly on, just as it always has done.

Christ's excellent advice to us is to take one day at a time, and never to worry about tomorrow. Following His teaching on that point is a great reducer of waiting-stress.

Waiting

We live upon the slopes of circumstance.
Sinister peaks that smoke and tower above life's
fragile tents,
Challenging us to wait while they decide
The trivial issues of our lives and deaths.
We try in vain to read our destiny within their
spirallings.
We need not wait for Fate,
Nor dance attendance on the Priests of Chance.
Destiny has no strange, capricious power to rule our
lives.
That power is God's: but in His wisdom and His
changeless love
He sets us free to choose, to carve our way
uncumbered
Through life's strange jungles of undreamed
adventure:
Onward and outward to the broad, bright plains,
Shining with golden opportunity.

Prayer

God of all courage and adventure, Lord of every
worthwhile action, loving and encouraging Creator
of all true opportunity and challenge, help us to use
our waiting time positively and never to be stressed
by it. Remind us that when one door shuts another
always opens, and so help us, Lord, to press on
again,
fired by Your gifts of hope that never dies and by
the high ambitions You have given us.
Amen

The Stress of Children and Young People

Children are wonderful: the loveliest possible companions. They inspire us to rise to heights we never thought we'd reach in order to do our best for them because we love them so much. But there are other occasions when even the best of deeply loved children can wear down the most patient and affectionate parents, guardians or carers. Children can demand so much care, attention and supervision that we just can't meet all their demands. Then a sense of our own failure -- however harsh and unjust the verdict we pass upon ourselves may be - merges with the stress generated by the children's needs and becomes very difficult to manage. At those moments it helps to remember that Christ, whose life and teachings provided a Master Class in love, was especially fond of children: "For of such," He said, "is the Kingdom of God." He who loves them so much, can help us to love them and cope with them just as He does.

Children

When we've comforted, cleaned them and fed them
Read them stories and joined in their play.
When we've wiped egg and jelly from tables,
And put their computer away,
When we've had all their friends round for parties,
And sung every nursery song twice,
When we've been to the park throwing snowballs
And slipped more than once on the ice,
When they won't go to bed when we ask them,
Because of their show on TV,
And we feel we could give them, or sell them
To the first alien space ship we see,
Than remember that Jesus loves children --
And the perfect example He set:
No matter how worn or exhausted,
We have to keep loving them yet.

Prayer

Most loving Lord, You always loved and welcomed
children during your years on earth with us. Help
us to follow your great example always to love them
as You did, to care for them, to protect them, and to
do all that we can to bring them to You.
Amen.

The Stress of Ageing

You still feel like an exuberant twenty-year-old inside. There are so many enjoyable and exciting things to do, so many places to go and so many golden opportunities to reach for: then you look in the mirror, or run back upstairs for something you've forgotten. The wrinkled face in the mirror is not one you recognise. The tired body that pants and creaks in protest when you ask it to take you upstairs does not match the effervescent idea-champagne of your mind. This is the stress of age, and there is only one remedy: *fight as you have never fought before*. You can hold the age-dragon at bay with the sword of courage, and the trusty shield of indomitable determination. Put on the strong armour of a nutritious diet and regular exercise. God has placed us in a strange and challenging world in which mind can overcome matter to a far greater extent than we realise. Let your mind lead the way: your body will follow it as surely as a faithful Squire follows his Knight into battle. Never give in. Never give up. Never lose your ambition. Never relinquish anything. Never stop trying. The twenty-year-old inside you is the real and eternal truth about your personality. The age-dragon is only a paper monster. Don't be afraid of it. Don't be deceived by it. Don't be stressed by it. You *can* overcome it with God's help.

The Age-Dragon

There's nothing that I can't achieve. There's nothing I
can't do.
With healthy food and exercise, I'll stay as good as new.
I'll fight as I have never fought to keep old age at bay.
Great God of Power Unlimited, help me to win the day.
Help me to make the very most of life's exciting stage -
Then with Your help I shall defeat
The Dragon of old age!

Prayer

Almighty Father, Lord of time and eternity, help me never to be stressed by age but to overcome it, and live life to the full to the very end. Divine Source of all power, give me the strength and energy I need to help those who depend upon me and who need such help as I can give them in Your Name, and for Your sake.

Amen.

The Stress of Travel

Going places can be fun. Travel can be great. Motorbikes, cars, trains, coaches, cycles -- or good old human feet -- it can be wonderful to go places whether we're in a glider, on horse-back, in a submarine or a wheelchair. That's the up-side of travel. It has its downside too. Traffic congestion can be frustrating and stressful. Train and bus delays can wind us up close to breaking point if we have to get to a certain place by a certain time. If one stage of the journey depends upon another, delays can threaten the entire travel plan. All too often we can do nothing except fume and put our blood pressure up when these stressful delays occur. Getting lost has a similar effect on us. The place we're anxiously trying to reach is effectively insulated from us by newly pedestrianised areas and one way streets, or, if we do manage to reach it, there's nowhere to park. Stress and pressure build up inside us again.

What can we do about it? If the appointment is a very important one, it's worth leaving really early. When everyone's depending on you to present the show, or to be the main celebrity guest, it's far better to reach the studio an hour early than to risk being even two minutes late.

Remember, every mode of travel and every route in God's Universe is ultimately subject to His unlimited power and love. It is infinitely better to ask for His help when travel becomes stressful than to give way to anxiety and frustration.

Travel

When roads are clear and lights are green,
We can enjoy each changing scene.
When roads are jammed and lights are red,
We wish that we could fly instead.

When skies are blue and sunshine's bright,
We're glad to travel on till night.
When skies are grey and rain pours down
The road is dull and so's the town.

When seas are gentle round the boat,
On peaceful waves it's good to float.
When raging gales lash billows' foam,
We hold our breath and pray for home.

When travel makes us tired and stressed,
We long to find a place to rest.
From north to south -- go where we will --
Our Father God goes with us still.

Prayer

Lord of every destination and of all the roads
between, be with us wherever and whenever we
travel. Free us from the stress of travel, give us calm
and peaceful minds, however difficult and
frustrating our journey may be. Remind us that the
only journey which really matters is our journey
home to You and to Your Kingdom of Everlasting
Joy. We ask it in the Name of Jesus Christ our Lord.
Amen.

The Stress of Public Appearances

It's a good thing for the world that we're all different. Some of us are naturally assertive, extroverted and supremely confident. We revel in public appearances. If we're show-business or media professionals, our stresses and anxieties begin to build up if we think we're not getting *enough* exposure. On the other hand, if we're naturally quiet, shy and retiring, the thought of having to appear in public or - horror of horrors - to *speak* in public, is one of the most terrifying ordeals we can imagine. It creates almost unbearable levels of stress and anxiety.

Deal with it as you would deal with any other type of stress: take it to God. The loving Father who created and sustains us knows infinitely more about us - and about how we function - than we can ever hope to learn about ourselves.

The audience are not critical or hostile. They're just normal, average people like us. They're sympathetic and friendly if a speaker's nervous or shy. Treat them as a group of caring friends and you'll be pleasantly surprised at the way your talk is received.

Facing the Audience - a Sonnet

I knew my speech by heart when I came in.
I heard the Chair announce my name, and then
My mind went blank, and I could not begin.
I drew deep breaths and counted up to ten.
The water sparkled down from jug to glass.
I drank it gratefully and tried again.
Somehow this awful moment had to pass.
Normality would soon return: but when?
The stress built up behind its fragile dam
Of brittle self-control and outward calm -
As vulnerable as sacrificial lamb -
My spirit longed for fragrant healing balm.
I launched one swift and desperate silent prayer:
And memory returned - my speech was there!

Prayer

Lord of all, great Reader of every human heart. You
know our strengths and weaknesses. You
understand, loving Father, just how difficult it is for
some of us to try to make a speech. Strengthen and
support us Lord. Help us to overcome our shyness,
our stress and our problems of appearing in public,
for Jesus' sake. Amen.

Irrational Fears and Phobias

There are enough real, tangible fears in this awesome universe. We don't need to manufacture any imaginary ones: the fear-market is glutted. Yet for so many people, phobias and irrational fears arise unbidden and strive to dominate our lives. These phobias are so widely known, and so many people are plagued by them, that most have acquired their own special medical, scientific names: like agoraphobia - the fear of open spaces and claustrophobia - the fear of being shut in.

Because of our wide-ranging and distinctive human differences, it is hard for the person who is *not* plagued by a particular phobia to empathise with the person who is, and to try to understand the stress which that friend's phobia is generating.

We can take positive steps to control and conquer our own phobias - if we have any - by attacking them with pure reason. Telling ourselves repeatedly that there is nothing rational to fear or dislike in the object of our phobia will help us to weaken its grip on our minds. If we ask for God's help with this, it will most assuredly be given.

The Phobia Sonnet

The dread of heights, of water, or the dark,
Can fill our minds with fears innumerable.
Some cannot bear the sight of flame or spark,
While others shun deep waters brimming full.
Who dreads the cat, the owl, or other birds?
The serpent's scales, the reptile, or the fish?
We tell ourselves such terrors are absurd:
To break their chains in our most fervent wish.
Like Sinbad and the Old Man of the Sea,
Each damning phobia grips and wears us down.
A different one, perhaps, for you and me:
Fear likes to dress in many a gaudy gown.
"Let not your hearts be troubled." God is near.
"Love that is perfect casteth out all fear."

Prayer

Lord of perfect and all-conquering love, grant us
that love which casteth out all fear. Help us so to
focus our minds upon You, and upon the needs of
others, that we shall have no room left for fear of
any kind, real or imaginary. We ask it in the name of
Christ, our loving and utterly fearless Redeemer.
Amen.

The Stress of Insomnia

The circular pattern of insomnia is a familiar enemy. First we find sleep is elusive. Then we tell ourselves that we *need* to sleep. Next we become increasingly fretful, anxious and stressed because sleep continues to avoid us. The more we worry about not sleeping, the greater our stress becomes, and the higher our stress level rises, the further we drive sleep away. For the insomniac, stress is massively dysfunctional. The first step is to shatter the popular illusion that sleep is essential and that failure to get the recommended amount each night will damage us in some way: *it won't*. Sleep patterns are not only highly individualistic and widely varied, they can change over time for the same individual. Sleep and boredom are close relatives: the person who is totally absorbed and fascinated by what he, or she, is doing will happily postpone not only sleep but meals as well. The keenly task-motivated man or woman manages perfectly well - he, or she, remains perfectly healthy without sleep for surprisingly long periods. The body usually has a good idea of what sleep it needs. Just relax. Never worry about your sleep pattern. You'll sleep when you really need to. If you want to encourage your sleep-trigger to operate, try soaking in a warm herbal bath and drinking a mug of warm milk before going to bed. Best of all, take the problem to God in prayer. Sleep will most assuredly come when you truly need it.

The Gentle Gift of Sleep

The hum of bees amid the flowers they love,
The ripple of the stream below the bridge,
The gentle cooing of the homing dove,
The cattle grazing by the meadow's ridge:
These are the welcome sights and sounds to keep
Within our minds upon their quest for sleep.
In perfect trust, in God we safely rest,
Then rise renewed to press on with our quest.

25

Prayer

Lord of all strength and energy, You are also the Lord of all gentle sleep and rest. Loving Father, You understand our every need far better than we understand ourselves. Take from us all stress and anxiety about sleep, so that we may always rest safely and peacefully in You, and rise refreshed and renewed, for the sake of Jesus Christ our Lord. Amen.

The Stress of Not Understanding

There are so many new and different things to try to keep up with in our modern world, that it is very difficult to understand them all. Every aspect of our lives is affected by this continual newness in one way or another. New things - even good and helpful new things - can generate stress. Where new things are difficult to understand, our stress increases dramatically.

There can be sudden organisational changes at work to which we find it very difficult to adjust. Friendly, reliable, trustworthy and dependable colleagues leave and we either have an increased work load or a personality clash with their replacements. We don't seem able to understand the new people -- and they don't seem able to understand us. Chronic disagreement is stressful. Let no-one try to persuade you that "creative conflict" exists in the workplace. Many years as a Management Consultant convince me beyond a shadow of doubt that any conflict of personalities is invariably negative and counter-productive as far as the organisation is concerned.

We can help to cure the stress that comes from our failure to understand people, places, systems and things by taking the time to learn. God has given us powerful minds which are more than capable of solving most of our problems, but they work best when we give them *time* to analyse the data and reach solutions. We also need to be strongly motivated towards problem solving. Time and prolonged mental effort are great allies in our war against the stress we feel when we don't understand something.

Incomprehension

We look towards the Universe's edge
To find that clouds of mystery bar the way.
Within our hearts we make a solemn pledge
That we will penetrate those clouds some day.
And piece by piece, our data we collect,
Arranging facts in academic line:
The cutting edge of human intellect
Will hew new theories from this data mine.
Give yourself time and motivation strong:
You'll solve the stressful problems that surround.
You'll understand these new things before long -
The unexplained becomes familiar ground.
Incomprehension's darkness turns to light:
Stress vanishes and everything is right.

Prayer

Lord of all wisdom and knowledge, Master of
Infinite Mystery, Designer and Sustainer of this
stupendous universe, we bring our problems to
You, knowing that You understand all things
perfectly and that You can and will help us to
understand those things which we cannot
understand now. Teach us that Your Perfect Wisdom
is sufficient for all our needs, through Christ our
Lord. Amen.

Work Stress and Business Worries

The Duke of Wellington is reported to have walked quietly and meditatively across the battlefield at Waterloo after his hard fought victory over Napoleon and said, "The only thing sadder than winning a battle is losing one." Had he been an entrepreneur instead of a soldier, he might have said, "The only thing more stressful than running a successful business is running an unsuccessful one." When an honest and able businessman, or woman, has done his, or her, best to keep a business running, and when that business has failed despite all the energy and intelligence that were put into it, the disappointment, stress and unhappiness are almost overwhelming. Yet it is nearly as stressful to run a business when things are going well. You don't have to be the proprietor or senior partner to feel that stress. The departmental head, the supervisor, the man or woman at the chalk-face actually *doing* the job on which the business ultimately depends -- *all* share the inescapable stress and responsibility which goes with business life in the twenty-first century. There are times when we think that everything depends on us - and we simply don't feel up to it. There is an appropriate old aphorism which is relevant here: *It all depends on me - and I depend on God!*

His strength is demonstrated best in our human weakness. When the stress of our role in business, commerce or industry becomes more than we can cope with, we need to remember that when we have honestly done all we can, God invites us to turn to Him for that vital extra *something* that we need to get us through.

Running the Show

Somebody has to do the job.
Somebody runs the show.
It's called responsibility -
It makes the business grow!
You know what's wanted urgently -
You've told the client: "Yes!"
But you're over your head with problems,
And you're desperate with stress.
When you don't quite seem to measure up
To the market's measuring rod -
Refer to Higher Authority
And take your stress to God.

Prayer

Lord of all, You handle everything in this vast, cosmic
creation, help me to handle the little bit of it which I see as
my responsibility today. Give me the strength, patience
and endurance I need to run this business, to complete
this difficult assignment, to fill this order, and to be fair,
honest, accurate and conscientious as I do it, for the sake
of Jesus Christ, our Lord.
Amen

Redundancy and Unemployment

This is an age of re-organisation, of down-sizing, of re-deployment and redundancy. Tragically, it is all-too-often the age of the almighty balance sheet and the cost-cutting efficiency expert. Human values are submerged in economic ones. People are the casualties when budgets are victorious. The stress of redundancy, re-deployment, and unemployment is very difficult to handle. You've done a good, worthwhile and significant job for years: suddenly you're told you're not needed any more. The trauma is devastating. From being a valuable member of a team doing an important job, you're told you're superfluous. You're unemployed.

The way to cope with this highly stressful situation is to see it for the cruel and evil fallacy it is. You are just as important and valuable as you have ever been. Your intrinsic worth as a person has not been diminished by one iota - and it never can be. You are a child of God. You are a unique part of His creation. The firm you once worked for thinks it can do without you: *God can't*. There is a unique place for you in His eternal plan and a home for you in His Eternal Kingdom: God has a vitally important vacancy which you *alone* can fill. If God thinks so highly of you - and you can be sure that He does - you should have that same high opinion of yourself. Ignore those who have made the cardinal error of making you redundant: prove them wrong. Go for every great new opportunity you can find - and go with God.

Redundancy and Unemployment

They've told you you're not wanted - they are wrong!
You're a key note in Heaven's glorious song.
The God who brought our Universe to birth
Has work for you to do for Him on Earth.
Shrug off the disappointment, hurt and stress:
Sharpen your sword and find some Great New Quest!

Prayer

Loving Heavenly Father, when we feel the hurt, pain and stress of being made redundant, and being unemployed, help us to remember that in Your perfect sight we have infinite value. Whatever the world says to us, You always love us, value us and want us. Give us the strength, courage, fortitude and resilience to go on seeking for new opportunities until we succeed. We ask it in the Name of Christ, our Lord. Amen.

Accommodation Problems and the Stress of Homelessness

A bright, warm, cheerful, secure, home environment is a rich blessing, and one for which we all strive. Far too many of our brothers and sisters are deprived of it. Being in a precarious, temporary, home situation, or one in which there is a chronic, tense atmosphere, is very stressful indeed. Even the wildest and most daring adventurers sometimes long for the comfort and security of a good, stable home. If we are to feel truly contented, safe and secure, we need a base, a den, our own personal, private fortress, or citadel, into which we can retreat, bar the door and hoist up the drawbridge.

The feeling of insecurity and of hovering over the abyss of homelessness are among the worst of all possible forms of stress.

There are national and local Government agencies, charitable organisations and Christian hostels which can help even in the direst cases. It is often much harder for most of us to accept help than to offer it to others: but it is just as much a part of true Christian charity to accept help graciously as it is to offer it generously.

Home

"Foxes have holes," the Saviour taught, "a bird of air its nest."
But He, the Son of God on Earth, had no safe place to rest.
He preached God's truth, and healed the sick. He helped the blind to see
He promised us a Heavenly Home with Him eternally.

Prayer

Most loving and hospitable Lord, help us to cope
with the terrible stress and anxiety of having
nowhere to live. Help us to find peace and security
in your Everlasting Arms,
even when we are sleeping in the street.   Please find
refuge, help and shelter for us here on Earth.
Builder of our Perfect and Eternal Home, help us to
reach it safely so that we may enjoy unending
happiness there with You and all those whom we
have loved on earth. We ask it for the sake of Christ
our Lord. Amen.

Financial Stress

Money is no problem at all when we have enough for our immediate needs, a reasonable amount put by for the proverbial rainy day and a little bit on top of that for a few harmless pleasures and minor luxuries. Money can become a problem when we have vastly more than we know what to do with, so that we inevitably begin to worry about it. Money is an infinitely worse problem when we don't have enough, when we are desperately stressed about how the rent, the electricity and the water bills will be paid, and where the next meal's coming from. Many of our brothers and sisters have to struggle with this monster of financial stress for many years - sometimes for the whole of their lives. Chronic poverty is a terrible and desperately stressful burden to try to bear.

There are ways in which we, ourselves, can fight this particular beast, as well as praying for God's help to overcome it. Careful thought and sound planning are always vital. We mustn't let financial matters drift. Work hard and think hard; make sensible economies without turning into the sort of creature Ebenezer Scrooge was before his conversion; and look for every good and honest way we can find to earn more, save more and spend less. Money management isn't easy. It's an area of life where we often need God's help. Never hesitate to ask for it - He is more willing to give than we are to receive.

Money

Lord, grant enough to pay our way - with just a bit to spare:
That means as much as food and drink: as vital as fresh air.
Too great a fortune brings distress and worries to our door -
But worse than that a thousand-fold: the curse of being poor.
Lord, save us from the miser's life, and hoarding wealth alone.
Lead us to help the ones whose needs are greater than our own.

Prayer

Most generous Lord, save us from the peril and
stress of poverty. Help us always to sympathise
with those who do not have enough, and make us
generous, willing givers. We ask it for the sake of
Christ our Lord, who gave everything -- including
His life -- for us. Amen.

The Stress of Owning Animals and Pets

One of our current owners is a very large, long-furred, black and white, feline gentleman, who occasionally condescends to come in when we open the back door and shout "Chilli" as loudly and invitingly as possible. He appears on the dining room window sill when he's ready to honour the house with his presence and indicates with an imperious "miaow" that one of his staff may now have the privilege of opening the back door, fetching his biscuits and turning on his gas fire for him if it's cold outside.

When all has been done to his satisfaction he will purr approvingly, curl up by the fire and sleep.

Another of our employers is Miranda, a very beautiful, very round-faced cat, who normally reigns from Jane's room but wanders the corridors matriarchally from time to time to satisfy herself that the rest of us are (a) working hard and (b) behaving properly.

Cats, dogs, horses, birds, hamsters, mice, gerbils, guinea pigs . . . The list is endless. Loveable pets are among God's richest gifts to us.

For 99.9% of their lives they are very effective stress reducers. They entertain us, soothe us and give us their love and loyalty. It's when they are injured or become old and ill that the stress comes in. We cannot bear to see them suffer, and we cannot bear to part with them. Very recently three of our greatly loved feline veterans: Tiggy, Jade and Minstrel all went to a better world through sheer old age. We still miss them terribly and grieve deeply for them. The stress of losing a much-loved pet of any kind is hard to bear. The more you loved them, and the longer you had them, the worse it is.

No loving human parent would deprive a child of a much-loved pet. God, our infinitely loving Heavenly Father, most certainly will not. God is pure love, and the nature of love is completeness. Heaven would not be complete for us without the animals we loved so much on Earth. God will make sure that we meet them all again in a place of perfect joy, exciting adventure and endless, abundant life with Him.

Tiggy

Your dish is empty now:
As empty as the quiet cat-shaped shell
We buried underneath the holly tree
When you went on.
Although we cannot see you any more
Or stroke your tiger stripes
The way we always did
To hear you purr,
And feel your fur against
A loving cheek,
As sure as God is God
We'll meet again,
Peter the fisherman who guards the gate,
Will see you don't go short
Until Death's tiresome quarantine
Restores you to our loving arms again.

Prayer

Most loving Creator and Sustainer of every living
thing in Your great universe, we know that you
would never separate us from the pets we love so
much. Keep them safe and happy with You until we
come to collect them to be with us forever in our
own little corner of Heaven. We ask it for the sake
of Him who told us how the Good Shepherd found
the lost lamb and brought it safely back, Jesus Christ
our Lord.   Amen.

Artistic and Creative Stress

They used to call it the fear of the blank sheet. Perhaps we should call it the fear of the blank screen today: the challenging vacuum, the aggressive emptiness which defies the writer or artist to fill it. That's one type of stress which plagues sensitive creative people. The other type is knowing that you have to produce -- *or else*. If you can't fill that blank screen or blank canvas, you can't fill your stomach either. Your artistry and literary talent pull you forward - your realism and sense of financial responsibility provide an additional impetus from behind. Between the gentle urgings of the Muses and the hefty hobnailed kick of financial necessity you have to overcome the dreaded blankness.

When you've painted the picture, sung the song, carved the statue, written the novel or collection of poetry, another type of stress sets in: *is it good enough?* Will the critics maul it, or praise it all the way into the prize lists? The thickest brazen collar and the toughest pachydermatous hide, will not provide total insulation from vitriolic critics. The strongest self-confidence and the biggest, brashest ego can occasionally be wounded. The wound may not show. A proud determination not to let the enemy know you're hurt may camouflage it from all but the wounded artist - but hidden or displayed, the wound still hurts like hell. The stress of trying to conceal it adds considerably to the load. God understands the anxiety of creation: the Perfect Creator knows the problems which imperfect creators encounter. Ask Him to carry you through it, and through the hurt which critics can inflict.

Creativity Sonnet

How can I match this perfect emptiness ?
So white the canvas and so blank the screen:
My finest words and brightest images
Will not succeed where emptiness has been.
What will the critics think about my work?
I try to tell myself I do not care,
Yet deep within me strange misgivings lurk;
I counteract anxiety with prayer.
The earth is green; the azure dome is blue.
God paints those fleecy clouds with thistledown;
Art is not art unless its aim is true:
The hand of God bestows the artist's crown.
Then fear no critics - nor the untouched blank -
When triumph comes, it's God whom we should thank.

Prayer

Lord of creation, Supreme Artist and Author of all good and perfect things, grant us a tiny share of your benign creative skill, that we may work in harmony with You to shape the world in accordance with your perfect plan and to colour it with kindness, love and fellowship.
We ask it for the sake of Christ our Lord.   Amen.

Family Stress

A family circle at its best can be a warm, loving, protective capsule of pure joy for all concerned. We need to respect one another's differences, to make generous allowances for them and to do everything we can to make everyone else in the family happy.

At its worst, because family members know one another so well and live in such close proximity, they can inflict deep, painful wounds upon one another - far more serious wounds than the external world can inflict.

The family can also generate more stress for its members than the outside world can throw at them. It is, therefore, essential for the family to be our strongest positive influence, an essential part of the anti-stress therapy God has provided for us. He has also given us the power to create family substitutes and family alternatives. We don't have to be relatives in the formal traditional sense in order to be a good and loving family in the spiritual and emotional sense. A good church, a good social club, a street full of good neighbours can come very close to the highest family ideals, if we all try hard enough, with God's help, to make it happen.

Families, Neighbours and Friends

When life is a mess, we can lighten the stress
With our families, neighbours and friends.
And when work is a bore, we can still do some more
For our families, neighbours and friends.
When money is short, and our ship's far from port,
We need families, neighbours and friends.
When our health lets us down and we can't get to
town
We've got families, neighbour and friends.
Though we're stressed to the bone, we don't bear it
alone -
There are families, neighbours and friends.
It's essential to learn how to make fair return
To our families, neighbours and friends.
So when they are in need, we will go at full speed
To help families, neighbours and friends.

Family Prayer

Father, Son and Holy Spirit, Divine and Perfect
Family of Triune Majesty and Sacred Mystery, hear
our prayer for human family life on the Earth which
You have made for us to enjoy together. Keep us free
from all family stress and conflict. Enrich and
increase our love for all our relatives and friends, so
that we may bear one another's burdens and reduce
one another's stress. Amen.

Mental, Physical and Spiritual Stress

God in His infinite wisdom has made every human being as a blend of mind, body and spirit. The physical part of our nature is the easiest to comprehend - and even that is amazingly complicated. Cells, tissues, organs and systems work together in a dynamic, biochemical symphony which plays the mysterious melody of life. With the right combination of exercise and diet, we can improve our physical bodies almost beyond recognition. It is part of God's loving plan for us that we should strive to make the most of the physical potential that He has given us. Health and energy are perfectly in tune with the will of God. But even the finest, fittest and most muscular body can experience stress and strain.

The mind - with its delicate rational and emotional components, and its conscious, subconscious and unconscious levels, seems more difficult to understand than the body. Our love, our ambition, our hopes and anxieties, our problem solving abilities and our restless human curiosity all dwell here. The mind is the mood factory where joy and misery lie partly assembled on adjacent benches. It is also the stress factory. Worry and fear are the industrial saboteurs who can wreck the mind's production line if we don't get them off the premises fast.

Spirit is the finest and most beautiful thing we have: the soul, the immortal essence which pervades everything else. It is the clearest reflection within us of the God who gave it. It is the spiritual part of us which is the true woman or man - spirit is what we really are. The mind and body which are bathed in spirituality will rise above the ordinary. If the spirit is stressed and troubled, that is the worst possible form of stress. He who made us and sustains us, offers healing and restoration for mind, body and spirit. He invites us to take each kind of stress to Him, to lay our burdens down at the foot of the Cross, and find His perfect peace and everlasting refreshment.

Mind, Body and Soul

(A Fanthorpean Sonnet has the symmetrical rhyme scheme
AA, BB, CC, DD, CC, BB, AA
so that the thought in the opening couplet is reflected
and emphasised in the final couplet.)

All praise and thanks to God whose loving arts
Created human nature in three parts.
The aching muscle, struggling with its quest,
The tired mind that fights on when it's stressed,
The soul that seeks for God, although beset
By doubt and failure, goes on seeking yet.
Body and soul, with mind -- all three aspire
To join the music of the heavenly choir.
God helps us to tear through temptation's net:
The greatest warrior is in Heaven's debt.
By saints and angels comforted and blessed,
We'll reach our haven harbour with the rest.
The battle over, Heaven's feasting starts:
All praise and thanks to God from grateful hearts.

Prayer

Omniscient Creator, perfect Lord of love and
wisdom, You have made all that we are, and all that
we can ever hope to be. Help and inspire us to do
the best that we can do, for You and for our brothers
and sisters. Grant us the physical strength, energy
and endurance which we need to fulfil the mind's
ideas and the soul's aspirations.   Amen.

When the weather is fine and wide highways are almost empty, there are few pleasures to equal riding a big, smooth Harley Davidson through gently rolling green hills. When visibility is close to zero on a hopelessly congested road and you're already late for a vital studio call, the road seems to have been made in hell, and all the other drivers apparently work there.

Tempers flare. Horns blare. Lights flash. Road rage hovers around like a hungry pterodactyl ready to strike. Blood pressure mounts. Litres of adrenaline flow. Road stress becomes intolerable. What can we do about it? No matter how important the appointment is, you and the hundreds of other delayed drivers are infinitely more important. Your safety, health and happiness - and theirs - are the first priority. The world won't end just because you're an hour or so late. Relax; take it easy; keep doing your best to get through - but don't let it stress you.

Most important of all, talk to God about it. He understands how important your next appointment is, how serious the delay can be, and how frustrating this traffic gridlock is.

Road Rage

Wipers attack the screen through heavy rain:
The mad conductor's batons which direct
This strange and frantic tune -
Discordant and cacophonous -
A symphony which no one wants to hear
And fewer want to play.
God help us to escape this lunacy.
Grant us that strength of mind
And deep tranquillity: steadfast and calm
While road rage and aggression
Surge, burst and threaten all around.
May they have no effect upon the steadfast soul.

Prayer

Grant us, O Lord, a sense of perfect calm and
fortitude, so when the angry stresses of the road
surround us, we neither fret nor panic, as once Your
first disciples did on storm swept Galilee. Help us
to hear You saying "Peace, be still," as they once
heard You say it, and may we be reassured and
comforted as they were then.   Amen.

The Stress of Human Love

A deeply loving, romantic relationship can be one of the richest blessings Earth can provide. The human urge to love and to be loved is so powerful and primeval that if it is misdirected it can cause ungovernable stress. Its potential for ecstatic joy or cataclysmic disaster is equally great.

The *deliberate* choice of celibacy under the sad delusion that the denial of one of God's greatest gifts is in some way pleasing to Him is unutterable folly.

Shakespeare understood romantic love: *Romeo and Juliet* tells the timeless tragedy of what he called 'star-crossed lovers' just as *Midsummer Night's Dream* and *The Tempest* provided happy-ever-after scenarios with romantic love as their central force.

Through the mystical power of love, through the God given inspiration of ecstatic human love, we can achieve the greatest of our aims and endure the worst of our hardships. When lovers are together, their totality is infinitely greater than the sum of its parts.

But the greatest surge of romantic love can never substitute for integrity and morality. To leave a loyal and loving wife or husband after twenty years to run away with an exciting new partner can never be condoned or justified on the grounds that this new romance was overwhelmingly powerful, was 'bigger-than-both-of-us' and somehow excuses betrayal and disloyalty.

To be faced with that level of stress is to be pierced by the horns of the grimmest emotional dilemma, and it is hell on earth. We can just about survive on the soul's bleak coral island if disappointment and regret over what-might-have-been are its only other inhabitants. The awareness that we have been treacherous and disloyal is a terrible and relentless predator. It will inevitably devour everything on the island -- including the transient joy of the illicit love from which it was born.

Prayer for Sad Occasions

The Star of Love

(A Fanthorpean Sonnet)

Love is the treasure, the immortal gem
Which gleams on every lover's diadem.
The deepest ocean and the highest peak
Listen in silence when they hear love speak.
The furthest aeon passed, or time to be --
Hour glasses against love's eternity.
The brightest star in the dark vault above
Pales insignificant beside true love.
God's glorious gift of love gives eyes to see
The golden towers of immortality.
Love is divine, ecstatic and unique:
The lasting joy which every heart must seek.
This flower of perfect joy blooms from love's stem:
Its fragrance is all sorrows' requiem.

The Prayer of Love

Lord of Perfect Love, You created the exquisite
pleasures and wonderful delights of romantic love
for us to enjoy. Help us always to fulfil our need of
that ecstatic human love which You have given us
within the bounds of integrity, honesty, loyalty and
commitment. Amen

The Stress of Keeping Secrets

Guarding a secret can seem harder than guarding a dangerous prisoner obsessed with escaping. In the matter of religious confessions, I'm strictly an old-fashioned Priest. If someone entrusts a secret to me in that sacred and solemn situation, it goes with me to the grave. But it isn't easy. Some secrets seem to have a life of their own -- the more important they are, the more volatile and dynamic they seem to be - and the harder they are to contain.

It can be stressful to be entrusted with a really explosive secret. You know perfectly well that if it's revealed to the wrong people, at the wrong time, in the wrong place, it will do untold damage. It's strangely similar to that sinister feeling which some vulnerable people get on cliff paths or the roofs of tall buildings.

Yet we have to hold on to it somehow. Trust is trust and integrity is integrity. The only One with Whom we are entitled to share those precious secrets which others have left in our safe keeping is God Himself. We may always take them to Him in prayer - along with the stress they bring: we would be wise to do so. He knows them already, of course, but discussing them with Him greatly reduces the stress we feel when we try to carry them alone.

When we are given the precious secrets of those who honour us by regarding us as trustworthy, we should always consider it a privilege. God will give us the strength to carry them safely. He can and He will reduce the stress of secrecy to a level that we can cope with if we ask Him.

Secrets

(A Fanthorpean Sonnet)

It wrestles like a champion to break free,
This secret with more strength than you or me.
Temptation beckons: "Go, fling wide the door -
And share it with a thousand ears and more."
Write it in blood upon the battlefield:
The deaths of those betrayed because we yield.
Temptation fails: the secret must remain -
If it escapes, integrity is slain.
In God's good time, all truth shall be revealed.
From His omniscience, nothing is concealed.
Into His loving heart, your secrets pour.
Divine forgiveness is your Father's Law.
No deed is done which his great eyes don't see -
Yet there are none as merciful as He.

Prayer

Loving and merciful Lord of all, we bring our stressful
secrets to You, as we pray for Your understanding and
forgiveness. Bear our secrets with Your omnipotent
strength, and teach us how to guard them against all
temptation. We ask it for the sake of Christ, our Lord.
Amen

The Stress of Indecision

The horns of a dilemma can be more dangerous than the horns of a mad bull. We often have to decide between the greater of two goods, or the lesser of two evils. It is never easy. A great and much admired friend once told me that when he was only six years old, he and his devoted parents were on a ferry boat caught in a terrifying storm. The boat was spinning helplessly in the torrent, and in grave danger of going down. His father was a non-swimmer. His mother swam well. He distinctly recalls his father saying: "Don't bother about me, darling. Save our son if you can." It would have been a heartbreaking dilemma for a loving wife and mother - but the sturdy old ferry stayed afloat somehow, and no lives were lost.

Once we have made a decision, it can be hard to put it into effect - but making the decision is often more stressful than the action that follows. It may be a career move. It may be a proposal of marriage. It may be a police officer's decision about whether to make an arrest, a jury's decision on guilt or innocence, or a judge's decision on prison or probation. The balance is often as delicate as one grain of sand in the scales of justice.

Decisions need time. Decisions need very careful thought and prayer. Decisions need God. He is the ultimate source of all true wisdom. Ask Him for help. It will most surely come, and as it comes the stress of the difficult decision making will go.

Deciding

I do not know the way I ought to go.
I can't decide upon which path to choose.
Each offers some bright hope of future gain -
Yet each contains some precious thing I'd lose.

Ambition trails its dusty net once more.
The lurid vampire, Fame, smiles from her lair.
Money and Status advertise their stock,
And Power offers the controller's chair.

Along the other path, Real Value stands,
Though dull and brown the garment that he wears,
While Love and Honesty walk hand in hand,
And Loyalty his True Friend's burden bears.

Prayer

Lord, in Your eternal, loving wisdom, guide us
through all the stresses and strains of our decision
making. Help us to choose what is right, what is
kind, what is loyal and true, good, holy and
unselfish. Help us to resist the glittering
temptations of the world, and to choose instead Your
eternal values. Amen

Stress in the Garden

Much fine prose and many great poems have been written about the beauty of trees and flowers. Gardens can be great sources of inspiration, peace, happiness, calm and tranquillity. Gardens are beautiful and wonderful places in which to pray and meditate. But we have to be honest and realistic. Gardens can also provide nightmare scenarios of weeds, slugs, wasps, flies, garbage, the smell of compost and manure - and endless hard work. The things we want won't grow. Nothing seems to stop the things we don't want from turning into primeval forests and jungles. Gardens at their worst can be stressful and frustrating. They are a remarkably accurate reflection of life itself. It has the potential to be good, happy and full of excitement, adventure, success and wonder. It also has the potential to be grim, disappointing, frustrating, exhausting, stressful, deadly boring and unspeakably sad.

What can our gardens teach us about tackling the problems of life?

First, we have to persist. We have to go on going on. We can beat the weeds and the pests if we keep on fighting them forever. There's no truce. There are no breathing spaces to let them rally their forces. Gardening is a constant battle - so is life.

Second, we need to be perpetual optimists. Believe that it will all come right in the end - and you're more than half-way to victory already.

Third - and most important of all - we need God. The Creator and Sustainer of all life knows everything there is to be known about plants and how to tend them - and about our human lives and how to live them. Ask regularly for his help in the Garden of your Life, and you will be very pleasantly surprised by the flowers and fruits that will grow there.

The Garden of Life

God make my life a garden
Where I may grow for You:
The flowers of love and kindness,
The herbs of what is true,
The stately trees of virtue
And fruits that I may share
With all who need my help, Lord,
To show Your loving care.

Prayer

Most loving and caring Lord, You prayed in the
Garden of Gethsemane, and You came back to us in
a garden after destroying death itself. Help us to
make our gardens places of beauty and peace, where
we can find You in prayer and meditation. Help us
also to learn from our gardens about how to cope
with the stresses and strains of life. Amen.

Stress in the Kitchen

Whether you're a commercial caterer or master chef cooking for a living, or a busy house-husband cooking for a career lady and your children, kitchens of all shapes and sizes can be stressful places. There's always something on the boil - literally and metaphorically - and it never has a considerate sense of timing. The interruption, or diversion, invariably coincides with the critical moment when you need to watch that particular pan like a hawk. Then there are cookers to clean, surfaces to wipe down, floors to wash, endless lines of crockery and cutlery to deal with -- and even the most effective modern kitchen gadgetry never quite seems to work *entirely* on its own. It's easy to get overheated in a kitchen: the over-stressed mind seems to sweat there as profusely as the body does.

In Jerome K. Jerome's *Three Men in a Boat*, Harris tells his two friends that the famous scrambled eggs he makes are unforgettably delicious. They beg him to prepare some for them and eagerly await the outcome. All that Harris eventually produces are a few badly burnt, yellowish, leathery fragments which are practically inedible. Most of us have made similar mistakes in our own kitchens from time to time.

Just like a garden, a kitchen can be the source of great beauty and pleasure. It can also be a notorious source of frustration, disappointment and stress. What can we do to improve things?

Taking our time is vitally important, and we have to be firmly realistic and practical about how much can be achieved in what little time we have available. Five minutes before rushing back to school will produce an acceptable sandwich: it won't produce a three course meal. God wants us to be equally realistic with our lives. If we make too many demands upon ourselves, nothing will work well. Things will boil over and much potential nourishment and goodness will be wasted. It is infinitely better to do one job well than to attempt three or four and ruin them all.

The Kitchen

A most dangerous place is a kitchen,
To be entered by only the brave:
For each pot and each pan can take over a man
And a cooker can make him a slave!

A most wonderful place is a kitchen,
To be entered by only the skilled:
There's so much we can learn from each kettle and urn -
It's a place for the bold and strong-willed!

A most beautiful place is a kitchen,
To be entered by only the fair:
Every delicate sauce, as a matter of course,
Is a masterpiece vivid and rare.

A most marvellous place is a kitchen,
To be entered by only the wise:
Where their meats and their sweets provide glorious treats
For the taste-buds as well as the eyes.

A most challenging place is a kitchen,
To be entered by only the strong --
Packed with lessons galore behind each cupboard door
And the stress of all that can go wrong!

Prayer

Lord of all true creativity and beauty, You made this
wonderful world of delicious and fragrant food for us to
prepare and enjoy, to sustain us and give us strength for
our constant battles.   Help us to learn the lessons of life
from our kitchens and our cookery, so that we can cope
with stress in the wider world outside.

Amen.

Stress in the Streets

Road rage is one thing: street stress is another.

Some of us actually *enjoy* being in crowds: football matches, theatres, pop concerts, packed parties, rush hours on the London Underground - the great hurly-burly of life itself is somehow reflected there in the lively movement and togetherness of the crowd.

Others of us avoid crowds like the bubonic plague. Thank God we're all different. For those who find crowded streets, shops, buses and trains difficult to cope with, the stress is severe. How can we handle it? Try reminding yourself that these are *God's* people. He made them. He sustains them. He loves all of them as much as He loves you and me -- and every other individual. A crowd is just a tightly packed, fast-moving collection of ordinary individuals like us.

Then there's the fear of crime and violence on the streets: drug dealers' gun gangs, muggers, pickpockets, racist attackers, lurching alcoholics and aggressive beggars -- and there never seem to be quite as many policemen about as we need. Walking to the corner-shop after dark can be a frightening and stressful ordeal for some. It is prudent to take precautions. Some city areas are undeniably more dangerous than others, and the vulnerable do well to avoid them when they can. But the world's streets and roads have always been dangerous places - the man whom the Good Samaritan rescued in the parable had been attacked by violent thieves -- and that was 2,000 years ago. Jesus Himself taught us that a strong man, well armed, can keep his house safe - but only until a stronger man overpowers him. The old sailors' proverb advises us to trust in God, but to row away from the rocks. That's the best answer to this kind of street stress: a combination of sensible precautions and absolute faith.

Streetwise

Pavements are hard and cold.
When snow and ice cover them
They can be treacherous and dangerous.
****

But selfish, stone-hearted men and women
Are harder, colder and more dangerous
Than frozen pavements.
****

The streets are stressful --
Even for the toughest of the streetwise.
So take great care
Of those who look to you for their protection -
And of yourself as well.
****

The caring, loving and protective people --
Who do God's will --
May warm these frozen pavements
Where the homeless lie.
Perhaps may also melt a little of the ice
That covers hearts and stones.

Prayer

Loving, caring and protective Lord, help us to walk
safely and wisely through the dangerous streets of the
world. Help us constantly to do Your work of
guarding and protecting those who need our strength
to support them in Your Name. Grant us warm and
generous hearts and show us where kindness - given
in Your Name -- can melt the ice of selfishness. Amen.

Stress in the Shops

Shopping is a constant, stressful struggle between what we want and what we can sensibly afford. As a sub-plot to the main battle, there is an on-going series of skirmishes between what we really *need* and what we *want*. Our genuine *needs* are relatively few - our *wants* are limitless. Wants are curious plants - they grow in hungry soil which they themselves produce. They're parasitic parasites which feed upon themselves. Income never grows at the same rate as wants - unless we have an inexhaustible oil-well or gold-mine in the back yard. We go into a supermarket with a carefully prepared list of essentials and come out with at least three extra items which were definitely not on that original list!

Shopping can also be very stressful and frustrating when it's impossible to find a parking space close to the shop you want to visit. Going from shop to shop unable to find the goods you want is also stressful and frustrating. We're all human, and shop workers can get tired and irritable at the end of a long shift, just as their customers can. It's stressful for both parties when that exhaustion and irritability rears its ugly head across a shop counter.

Patience, understanding, tolerance and unselfish kindness are the keys. Treating one another as we ourselves would like to be treated is what Jesus taught us to do. It remains the best antidote to stress.

Shopping

I should have walked or caught a bus
It isn't very far.
I've passed the shop a dozen times:
I still can't park the car.
But when I find a parking space
And trudge back to the shop,
They don't have half the stuff I need
And I've no time to stop.
I spend on several *other* things
I really don't require:
My credit card jumps out as if
My wallet is on fire!
It can be so frustrating
When the shops are selling stress.
The Internet's a better way
Of buying things, I guess.
But then there's all the worry
Of the hackers and the sly:
If they can steal your number
They will drain your credit dry!
So fill life's shopping trolley full
Of loving thoughtfulness.
Unselfishness and kindness are
The goods which God will bless.

Prayer

Creating and sustaining Lord, everything that we
have and everything that we are comes from You.
Nothing that is made, and sold in shops, would be
there without Your creative and sustaining power.
Help us to make the most of our shopping and to
enjoy it, free from stress. But keep us ever mindful
of the needs of others, and help us to share the good
things of life with those in need. Amen

Educational Stress - School and University

It's a hard, tough, competitive world. Many of us spend far too much precious time preparing to jump through academic hoops of one sort or another in order to wave a piece of paper which says we've done it. The world is qualification crazy. Alexander the Great and Julius Caesar never went to a military academy. Jesus never attended a theological college in order to impress the disciples by wearing his collar back to front. Neither did Moses nor Elijah. Socrates and Plato did not possess diplomas to prove that they were Doctors of Philosophy - but their philosophical thoughts were sublime. It's your innate ability, intelligence and confidence that still matter most. The world urgently needs weaning away from its obsession with the delusion that training courses achieve very much, and from its fascination with impressive looking bits of paper which are worth little or nothing in the final analysis. (That's not sour grapes: I do have a few of my own! I too got well and truly caught in the rat race for status symbols and qualifications!)

But the stress they induce is enormous: research papers, examinations, dissertations, theses, vivas, time limits and page after page of rules and regulations.

Throw out your academic stress.

The world being what it is, we all have to fight like wildcats to get to the top - and then we have to fight like tyrannosaurs to stay there!

You, your personality, and your *ability* are what matter: work as hard as you can for all the academic and professional qualifications you can get - but don't be deceived by them. It is men and women who matter. It is loving hearts and generous minds that make the world a better place. Achieving your academic goals is useful - but never make the mistake of being stressed by the work they entail. You matter far more than the letters after your name. God reads your heart: he doesn't ask about your academic qualifications.

Academia

(A Fanthorpean Sonnet)

I have revised until my neurones ache -
I find I can no longer stay awake.
I've read until my retinas are sore --
I just don't feel like reading any more.
I want to pass. I want to qualify.
I've got to do my best. I have to try.
The competition in the world's grim race
Dictates this academic paper-chase.
Blue oceans beckon under the blue sky.
I'm working at my desk: I wonder why.
I take a pace across my study floor.
My fingers reach towards that tempting door.
Then I return again for Duty's sake -
To face the next exam I have to take.

Prayer

Lord of all knowledge, all wisdom and all skill, You
look into our hearts rather than into our academic
records. Help us always to do our best with the
knowledge that we have to acquire and the skills
we have to learn, but teach us that there are more
important things in Your universe, such as love and
compassion, and save us from academic stress.
Amen.

Religious Stress

The corruption of the best is the worst. All true religion comes from God and can be our greatest source of joy and peace. It is the sure road to everlasting happiness. To find eternal fellowship and communion with God and our brothers and sisters is the zenith of the soul's quest. To glimpse the goodness, the love and compassion of God -- and to *know* that in Him there is perfect and endless joy beyond our wildest imaginings -- is the heart of all genuine religion. *All* faiths which teach such fellowship, tolerance, love, joy, peace and eternal life are His creation -- by whatever name they call Him. This true religion calms and heals all our stress.

Tragically, there are several very dubious *things* which call themselves religions -- but are a million light years from the God of goodness, mercy, truth and love who created and sustains our universe. There are pernicious cults and narrow sects which teach exclusiveness, enmity, isolation, intolerance and a crippling Puritanism more restrictive than the minuscule mind of the worst Pharisee could ever have concocted. Their dangerous and totally erroneous teachings can create exceptional stress in the minds of the vulnerable.

Happily, there is a reliable cure for the stress they bring.

Every genuine, God-given religion teaches and practises warm and welcome inclusiveness, love, tolerance, mercy and kindness. Because God is good and because God loves us *all*, every true religion aims to make its people happy and free. That is the acid test. If a *thing* calling itself a religion fails to fit that profile, reject it. Don't let it misrepresent God to you, and don't let it cause you any stress. It is based on a fallacy, and may safely be ignored.